small-circle jujitsu

by wally jay

small-circle jujitsu

by wally jay

Editor: Mike Lee
Graphic Design: Sergio Onaga
Photography: Doug Churchill

©1989 Ohara Publications, Inc.
All rights reserved
Printed in the United States of America
Library of Congress Catalog Card Number: 89-42904
ISBN 0-89750-122-5

Second Printing 1989

OHARA 🔲 PUBLICATIONS, INCORPORATED, BURBANK, CALIFORNIA

Dedication

I would like to dedicate this book to Ken Kawachi, Henry S. Okazaki, Jimmy Mitchell, James Harada, Buck Kam Thom, Henry Peters, and Professor Juan Gomez. I also dedicate this book to my wife Bernice who encouraged and assisted me 100 percent, especially during the frustrating periods of my long career. All these people were my role models. I looked up to them and they gave me direction in my life—confidence and security.

—W.J.

Acknowledgement

Kokua is a Hawaiian term that describes a genuine regard for fellowship—of treasured help and friendship. So, it is with kokua that I acknowledge the following people who have made this book possible. Many thanks to Dan Inosanto for writing the foreword; to my friend M. Uyehara, who kindly endorsed and encouraged the idea for this book; to Mike Belzer and Keith Thomas, who took the punishment as the "bad guys"; Diane Hughes for executing the women's self-defense techniques and applications; to Jon Funk, Mike Belzer, and Kregg P. J. Jorgenson for their valuable assistance in preparing the manuscript; and to all of the people behind the publishing scene who contributed so much as well.

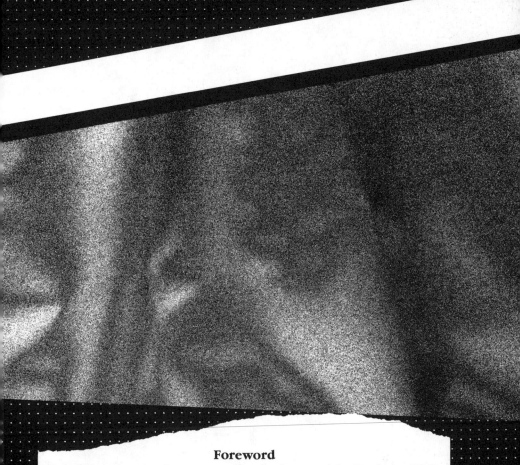

Foreword

It gives me great pleasure to write the foreword for Professor Wally Jay's book. He is a man I greatly admire and respect. His innovation and contribution of small-circle theory jujitsu will go down as a milestone in the history of martial arts.

Jay is highly respected, not only in the judo and jujitsu fields, but in the karate and kung fu worlds as well. In the last five years, whenever Jay has been in the Los Angeles area, my students and I have enjoyed attending his seminars. He is a man who is highly gifted, highly knowledgeable, highly creative, and highly innovative. But, more importantly, as a human being, he remains humble and ever helpful, sharing his knowledge unselfishly with all who attend his seminars.

Jay's creativeness and innovations in the art of jujitsu remind me in many ways of my instructor, the late Bruce Lee. Jay has been a great inspiration to me in my martial art pursuit, and I find him to be a pillar in the martial arts world.

—*Dan Inosanto*

About the Author

Professor Wally Jay is a grandmaster of jujitsu in America. He is a tenth dan in jujitsu and a sixth dan in judo. In 1969 he was inducted into BLACK BELT magazine's Hall of Fame. Born in Honolulu, Hawaii, on June 15, 1917, of Chinese descent, Jay spent his early years as a sheltered and frail child. At the age of 11, he turned to a community boxing program in the hope of gaining much needed confidence, direction and sense of personal security.

Under Jimmy Mitchell he learned the basics of boxing and a great deal more. Perhaps this is where he learned how great an impact instructors can actually have on their students—a lesson not lost on the talented Chinese-Hawaiian over the years, nor forgotten as he progressed through his martial arts studies.

In 1935 Jay turned to jujitsu under Paul Kaelemakule. Then in 1938-39, while attendinng Oregon State College, he studied boxing under coach Jim Dixon. By 1940, he was back in Hawaii, studying jujitsu. This time however it was under the tutelage of Juan Gomez, a top disciple of Henry S. Okazaki. By 1944, Jay had received his first-degree black belt in *danzan ryu* jujitsu and the following year was awarded his second-degree black belt along with his instructor's certificate from Gomez. Since it was mandatory for the new instructors to know massage and how to care for injuries, Jay also received his masseur's diploma from Okazaki.

It was during this time, too, that the young martial artist began studying judo under Hawaiian champion Ken Kawachi. It is Kawachi Jay credits with stressing the use of decisive wrist action that would later become one of the primary focal points in his small-circle theory jujitsu.

In 1950, Jay moved from Hawaii to Northern California where he began teaching judo. In the first few difficult years, he went on to excel in judo as an instructor and a coach, so much so that within a decade he had produced many local, regional, national and international champions in the traditional sport. By the early 60s Jay received his third-degree black belt rank in judo and was also named Judo Coach of the Year.

In 1962 Jay attracted the attention of a 22-year-old martial artist from Seattle named Bruce Lee. Lee was amazed how someone with little formal training in judo could go on to produce champions. However from the many long hours that Lee spent at Jay's *dojo* (training hall) with friend Jimmy Lee, the legendary martial artist saw the value of Jay's broad background in the fighting arts. Jay had adopted various techniques from boxing, wrestling, judo, kung fu, weightlifting and jujitsu and brought them together in what he called his small-circle theory jujitsu. Like Jay and his innovative instructors before him, Lee too knew that talent, technique and style knew no traditional boundaries and that excellence carried no single banner or flag. The three martial artists spent many long hours exchanging theories, fighting principles, and techniques, and over the following years a strong bond of trust and friendship developed.

As their reputations grew they remained friends and while Bruce Lee went on to take Hollywood, Hong Kong, and the martial arts world by storm, Jay established the ten principles that would set his mark in the world of jujitsu.

Since 1979 he has devoted all of his time to small-circle instruction, holding clinics in England, France, Norway, Sweden, West Germany, Holland, Singapore, Tahiti, Costa Rica, Mexico, Australia, New Zealand, Scotland as well as throughout the United States and Canada.

Jay was also the team captain of the United States representative team that took part in a cultural exchange program to the People's Republic of China. His exhibitions with Jim Silvan at the International Wushu Championships in Xian, China, in 1985 drew high praise and applause from those present. It was after that demonstration that Jay was singled out by three prominent Asian sports magazines, and, as a result, was later invited to return to China.

From his lifetime of contributions to jujitsu and the martial arts, Jay has received numerous honors and awards. He's a recipient of the National

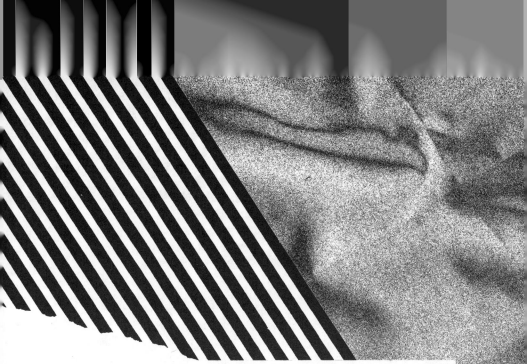

AAU Bud Estes Pioneer Memorial Award, has had a classroom named after him in Alameda, California, and, in 1965 was named the city's Man of the Year. For his efforts to his community Jay also received the Mayor's Medallion, joining such prestigious company as the late President John F. Kennedy and the late Minnesota politician and former Vice-President Hubert Humphrey.

In 1982 he was honored at a dinner in Waikiki, Hawaii, by former students with a long list of notable friends in attendance, including: Richard Kim, Ed Parker, Pat McCarthy, Ken Kawachi, Don Jacob and Juan Gomez. Leonard Lim, representing the Governor of California, presented Jay with a special Govenor's Proclamation honoring his service and contributions to California. With all these honors and awards the truly humble and talented martial artist remains firm in praising the many other pioneers in the field who have helped or influenced his own career—pioneers, who Jay says, deserve recognition as well.

In this regard Jay is behind a drive to find a sponsor to support a "Jujitsu Hall of Fame" in order to recognize those who have contributed so much to the betterment and proliferation of this fighting art. Jay is sincerely interested in giving something back to the art he feels has given him so much.

Besides an active and full traveling seminar schedule Professor Wally Jay serves as the technical advisor to a number of national and international jujitsu organizations and associations. He is a grandfather several times over and presently resides in Alameda.

IMPORTANT NOTE
The Rules of Safety at the Dojo

Learning jujitsu is as safe as learning volleyball, baseball, or tumbling if the rules of safety are heeded. Jujitsu teachers are safety minded because they are involved in the study of how injuries occur. Using this knowledge, they can advise you how to prevent these injuries. Every full-fledged jujitsu teacher knows revival techniques and how to treat minor injuries. Following are the common rules of safety:

• When your partner taps the mat, your body, or his own body more than once, he is letting you know that he is yielding. Release pressure but maintain the hold.

• He may yell *maitta*. This means he wishes to yield. Release pressure but maintain the hold with control.

• Do not horseplay in class. There is a danger of hurting others besides yourself and your partner.

• It is the thrower's responsibility to see that the mat is clear before throwing.

• In the application of joint lock holds, once the hold is tight, apply pressure slowly until your partner submits, then release pressure. Develop the feeling of sensitivity.

• Do not practice strangulation or choking techniques unless a qualified instructor is present.

• Do not throw a beginner unless the instructor gives his consent.

• Release the hold completely if your partner quickly moves in the wrong direction of escape. His countermove may cause him injury. Be considerate.

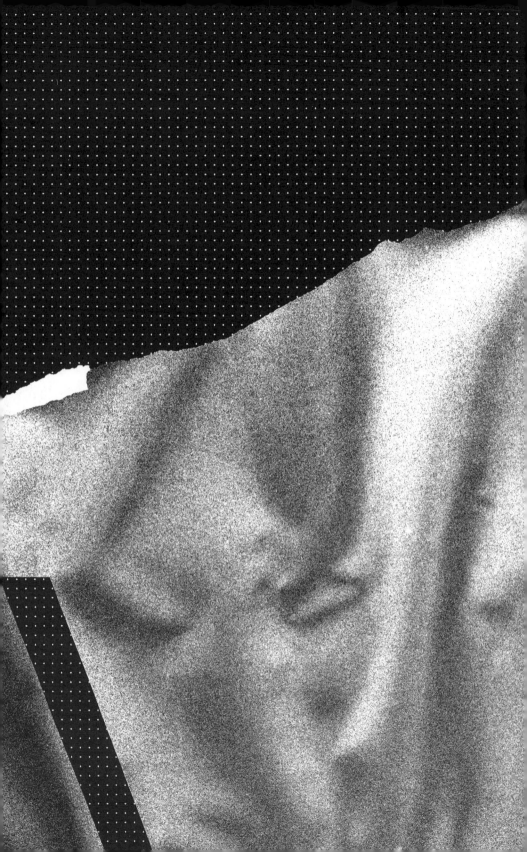

Contents

Henry S. Okazaki (left) and Wally Jay (right).

Chapter 1
THE STORY OF SMALL-CIRCLE JUJITSU

Henry S. Okazaki, founder of the *kodenkan* jujitsu system, moved to Hawaii from Japan at the age of 17. Because of ill health, he began studying jujitsu under Kichimatsu Tanaka at the Shinyu Kai Dojo. Exercise, training, and fighting improved his health and attitude so much that it spurred him on to further his study of judo and jujitsu, as well as other fighting art disciplines. He studied under masters of the *yoshin, kosagabe*, and *iwaga* jujitsu systems, as well as studying Okinawan karate, Filipino knife fighting, *lua* (the Hawaiian art of self-defense), the art of throwing a Spanish dirk, boxing, wrestling and even kung fu.

In 1924, Okazaki toured Japan to further his study of various jujitsu systems. There, he learned restoration massage and resuscitation techniques. At the Kodokan he received his third-degree black belt in judo.

On his return to Hawaii he continued his trade as a masseur and taught judo and jujitsu on the island of Maui. From his extensive studies he recognized the strong need to upgrade the techniques he learned, so he began to experiment and blend the techniques he had acquired. Okazaki's system developed into a syllabus of practical fighting arts.

In 1930, Okazaki moved to Honolulu to resume his career as a physical therapist and soon earned a remarkable reputation for the amazing results of his treatments. It was also about this time that he came to know a renowned therapist named Peter Baron who taught him how to operate a commercial studio and the techniques of Swedish massage. In appreciation, Okazaki did the unthinkable—he offered to teach Baron jujitsu. In those days, judo and jujitsu were taught to the Japanese only. Systems and styles were closed to all but a select few.

Indebted to Baron and realizing that the techniques of self-defense were universal, Okazaki subsequently offered to teach any person regardless of age, race, creed, sex, or handicap. Defying the traditionalists, Okazaki, for a time, was ostracized. He had broken tradition by teaching non-Japanese. However, he took consolation in his belief that knowledge transcended borders and that the martial arts belonged to those who needed them. Okazaki named his school Danzan Ryu in gratitude to Wo Chong, a Chinese who, like Okazaki, had broken tradition by teaching Okazaki, a Japanese, the Chinese art of kung fu.

Before long Okazaki's dojo flourished in many districts of the island—during and after World War II. The Army and Navy YMCA in Honolulu held classes for American service personnel, producing many black belts and instructors. After WWII, Okazaki's disciples returned to the United States where they opened their own schools.

In 1939 Okazaki founded the American Jujitsu Guild, which he changed in 1943 to the American Jujitsu Institute. Jay was a charter member of the latter organization. The institute celebrated its 45th year under the direction of President Sam Luke in 1988. The Okazaki splinter groups that were organzied in the United States are Jujitsu America at San Bruno, California; Hawaiian Jujitsu System at Jacksonville, Florida; American Judo and Jujitsu Federation at Chico, California; Kodenkan Danzan Ryu of Dayton, Ohio; Southern California Jujitsu Association; and the Kodenkan Yudanshakai of Tucson, Arizona.

In 1947, Okazaki sponsored the first judo tournament after World War II. The powerful Hawaiian judo *yudanshakai* men won all of the places convincingly. Jujitsu dropped to a new low after the defeat. After that embarassing and devastating defeat, Okazaki made plans to send for judo instructors from the Kodenkan Judo Institute. His plans did not materialize because of his untimely death in 1951.

However, from the defeat at the hands of the yudanshakai a valuable lesson was learned. The jujitsu men realized that learning the sport of judo was necessary and its science would enhance jujitsu. The lesson though

Henry S. Okazaki (left) and Juan Gomez (right).

would be costly. Many students of jujitsu switched completely to judo after the defeat while others struggled and fought to hold on and endure. A handful of those who went over the judo did well and then returned to jujitsu bringing their new found knowledge with them.

In the decades of the 1950s and 60s, several schools of jujitsu affiliated themselves with Hokka Judo Yudanshakai, the Northern California judo black belt association. At the beginning, the Okazaki clubs were no match for the tough California *judoka* (judo practitioners). Humiliated but proud, these instructors encountered difficult times in the transition from jujitsu to judo. They showed improvements at each succeeding judo meet, however, and several years later were able to hold their own against the top clubs of the Hokka Judo Yundanshakai. For the jujitsu/judo people it was a great victory because the Okazaki men had two diciplines now, judo and jujitsu knowing that each enhanced the other.

Over the years Okazaki's dream of producing outstanding competitors became a reality. His determined students fought overwhelming odds to be able to produce winners in local, regional, national and even international levels.

These students who went on to become the standard bearers were Ramon Ancho, Toru Tanaka, John Chow-Hoon, Tony Gonzales, John Cahill, Francisco Limbago, Bill Montero, Richard Takamoto, Don Montero and myself.

Perhaps Okazaki's most outstanding protege is Willy Cahill, coach of the United States World Judo Team, who has one of the most impressive records in judo in the United States. Cahill is presently chairman of the standards board of Jujitsu America.

Jujitsu Styles in America

The art of jujitsu in America has moved up to a very respected position on the martial arts totem pole during the years following World War II. In the 1940s and through the 60s, most of the schools came from traditional systems. Today, the United States has many schools of jujitsu and many splintered from the traditional styles.

Jujitsu schools in the United States generally began with the traditional styles such as *kito-ryu, kodenkan, hakko-ryu,* and *sosuishi-ryu* to name just a few. Initially, they were taught by Oriental instructors or Americans who had studied it in Japan and upon their return home set up schools of their own. Periodically, some returned to Japan for further study and advancement.

The first and second generations of teachers generally teach the traditional forms as taught by their instructors. Initially, it was one way they showed their loyalty, respect and, appreciation. But as each succeeding generation of teachers became leaders, they tended to modify the traditional arts, perhaps feeling that the traditional methods were irrelevant to their time or immediate needs. They adapted the most efficient techniques possible in order to add to their repertoire, maintain combat preponderance, or gain combat supremacy. This evolutionary cycle still continues.

Such was the case with the formulation of Jujitsu America in 1978. With conflicting ideologies and methodologies, the stateside regions of the Hawaiian based American Jujitsu Institute could not live up to the traditional expectations. Willy Cahill, John Chow-Hoon, Carl Beaver and I seceded to form Jujitsu America. The Hawaiian leaders wished to perpetuate the traditions of the kodenkan system while the statesiders, being modernists, wanted to update and improve their fighting skills to reflect certain modern realities.

The American standards of jujitsu are among the very best in the world today. There are many pioneers whose contributions have enhanced American jujitsu; such as Antone Pereira, Siegfried Kufferath, Antone Gonzales, John Chow-Hoon, Willy Cahill, Michael de Pasquale, Sr., Florendo Visitacion, Moses Powell, Juan Gomez, Ramon Ancho, Larry Greene, Dennis Palumbo, George Kirby, Jonathan Stewart, Toru Tanaka and Robert Crosson, as well as numerous others.

Evolution of Small-Circle Jujitsu

I studied judo during World War II under Hawaiian champion Ken Kawachi, a 135 pounder who had no trouble throwing three professional wrestlers weighing from 230 to 240 pounds, and he was equally effective grappling on the mat. My admiration for this great champion's technical skill led to a mutual friendship that has lasted a lifetime. I studied for two years under Ken Kawachi, from 1942 to 1944, I was still a white belt. During the war years, there were no organized judo tournaments, so I never had the opportunity to enter a judo tournament. The embryo of the small-circle theory came from this Hawaiian champion who was a master in the use of wrist action.

In 1953, I entered my team for the first time in the Northern California judo competition. The team was beaten by the tough Californians easily. The highest ranked instructor made a disparaging remark about "Wally Jay's judo," and all the instructors sitting on the stands with me joined in with their hearty laughter. Humiliated, I left the tournament with a silent

Ken Kawachi

vow to return when I was able to produce winners.

I did research. After a layoff from judo competition for a year during which I began to institute the results of my research, the team began to win some of their matches, and there was a marked improvement shown. I knew I was on the right track, and the method I called the small-circle became my obsession. Unlike the big circular movements of the traditional styles in which force is exerted during a hold by either pushing or pulling, I began to use a simultaneous push and pull.

Wrist action is the key to the small-circle. While the hand executes the hold, additional pressure is applied by flexing the wrist so the thumb pushes forward and the fingers pull back, thus exerting torque in the tightest possible arc. What results is an intensification of pressure on the opponent's joint, less time for him to react, less room for escape, and an increase in the amount of pain.

I also spent much of my time thinking about improving and blending moves of other sports. Small-circle jujitsu, taking its name from the small-circle method of executing holds, became a complete system of jujitsu, as I blended my knowledge of jujitsu, weightlifting, kung fu, aikido, wrestling, and Western boxing, complemented by the powerful wrist action emphasized by Kawachi.

I could see improvement at each succeeding meet. The team eventually became a winnng team. In 1960 I was voted Northern California Judo Coach of the Year by Hokka Judo Yudanshakai. The small-circle principles applied to judo competition were successful. In the 60s and 70s I produced national champions and team winners in Hawaii, Canada, USA, and Mexico. The scorn shown by the top-ranked instructors back in 1953 spurred me to find the winning combination which was small-circle jujitsu.

In 1978 I began to devote most of my time to teaching jujitsu self-defense in many countries, promulgating small-circle jujitsu worldwide.

Ten Principles of Small-Circle Jujitsu

Following are the ten principles that form the basis of small-circle jujitsu. They follow the laws of sports science, and through many years of research, have enhanced the science of jujitsu.

• *Balance.* Balance is perhaps the most important principle in any sport. The basic strategy of judo, for instance, is to keep your opponent off balance while maintaining your own. By keeping your own balance, you will have use of your maximum power while your opponent uses part of his energy trying to regain his balance. The more off balance he is, the more strength he will need to recover.

• *Mobility and stability.* Your center of gravity plays an important part in the principle of mobility and stability. Lower your center of gravity and you will achieve stability; raise your center of gravity and you will gain mobility. The hub of your action is at your midsection. When your center of gravity rises, you lessen your stability and increase your mobility, and vice versa.

Your mind can also control your center of gravity. Try these exercises for example. Lift your partner up slowly holding him around the waist. If your partner thinks of riding an elevator going upward with high speed, his body will be easier to lift. Lift your partner again. If he concentrates he is riding an elevator going downward, his body will be more difficult to lift.

For mobility move on the balls of your feet, and when pivoting, your knees should be either above or beyond your toes, and not directly over your heels. For stability, lower your body slightly. Stability is essential in punching or throwing.

• *Avoid the head-on collision of forces.* To avoid the full power of your opponent's attack, avoid the head-on collision of force by evading, deflecting, blending, or redirecting. Unlike other systems of martial arts training where you pivot in toward the opponent, this principle is just the opposite. As in all small-circle moves, always pivot away from the opponent when blending, redirecting, or evading. Try to evade the opponent's striking force by stepping back. Move 45 to 90 degrees to the left or right, or move laterally left or right.

• *Mental resistance and distraction.* Everyone has the ability to mentally resist pain. Try this with the bent elbow wrist lock applied on you by a partner. As the hold is applied, concentrate on the spot where the pain is felt. Imagine that there is a flywheel spinning at high speed at the spot, going in the opposite direction, which is counterclockwise. Do not use physical resistance, but remain calm and relaxed as you give your total concentration. If you are able to go into deep concentration, you will be surprised to find that you will feel no pain. If however, someone were to slap you on your wrist, causing you to lose your concentration, you will feel immediate pain. This also points up the vital part that the element of distraction plays in self-defense.

Distraction of the opponent's concentration is important when executing a counterattack. During the application of a technique when resistance is met, distract your opponent by attacking the weak areas of the body. This leaves him with less power and a split second loss of concentration. An unexpected shout or grunt may also allow you sufficient time to escape or counter. A sternum strike while simultaneously executing a wrist lock hold, for instance, or a kick to the shin while escaping a lapel grab, or a pinch to the inner thigh of someone using a bear hug on you may enable you to gain control of the fight more readily.

• *Focus to the smallest point possible (proper direction of force).* In transmitting the maximum amount of force and producing maximum pain, focus plays a vital part. Try to pinpoint pain to the smallest base possible. Transmission of energy to a wide base means that the energy is distributed over a larger area and less energy is directed to the point where the pain should be felt.

Be accurate with the direction of force. All small-circle techniques employ dual action of the wrists, pulling in with the fingers and pushing with the thumbs. Learn to use the extended arm movement in conjunction with this wrist action. With locks such as the bent elbow wrist lock, use the centerline (from throat to solar plexus) as the target of application.

Proper gripping when executing the technique is also very important. Learn where the fulcrum is and pull in toward your own body to keep the opponent in maximum pain.

• *Energy transfer.* An example of energy transfer is the application of the reverse arm bar, using your knuckles against your opponent's tricep tendon. First, use a heavy palm by pressing your palm heavily against the opponent's forearm below his elbow. Then, transfer the energy from there to the point of focus above the elbow, driving your knuckles directly into the tendon of the tricep. This energy transfer breaks your opponent's resistance more effectively than if you were to apply force to the area of focus immediately. His weak resistance is caused by applying the heavy palm below the elbow and then transferring the energy above the elbow. Kai Sai (Chris Casey) a leader in Chinese martial arts, explains that the opponent's inability to resist is due to "*chi* bleeding" caused by the energy transfer. When your palm is placed heavily agianst the back of the forearm below the elbow, the opponent's chi meets to resist the force at the opposite side, the front of the forearm. This leaves the rest of the arm above the elbow without sufficient chi to resist. Then when the energy is transferred there with the knuckles, the arm bar is easily set. Energy transfer is effective if the distance of transfer is short.

• *Create a base.* "Creating a base" is a new phrase specific to small-circle jujitsu. Whenever there is a lot of play in the hold you are executing, create a base to stop the extra play of the fingers, wrists, or any locks on the limbs. At one of my clinics, a young girl who was very supple and flexible felt no pain when a finger lock was applied on her. Her finger was able to bend all the way back with no pain. I created a base by placing my palm under her hand, restricting the amount of play, and she quickly submitted. You can create a base by using any surface to restrict the amount of movement the opponent may have, using your thighs, body, head, wall, floor, etc.

• *Sticking, control and sensitivity.* Sticking with your opponent during the application of a hold or a series of holds is vital. To counter any resistance or escape attempt, you must keep in constant contact with your opponent during the flow from one technique to another. This requires sensitivity.

To develop sensitivity, you must learn not to "muscle" the application of the hold. You must relax to feel the slightest movement by the opponent, sensing its direction and quality. This is the most difficult art to develop, but with sufficient practice it can be mastered. After it is mastered you will be able to sense your opponent's intentions instinctively, enabling you to decide what countertechnique to apply to maintain control.

• *Rotation momentum.* Rotation momentum is one of the major types of movement in small-circle jujitsu. Okazaki demonstrated this back in 1944. It is a method of creating strong off-balancing moves as a preliminary to throwing the opponent. By holding the opponent with both hands, you circle both hands in the same direction. One hand pulls while the other pushes. As the opponent leans to oppose your influence, you circle back, adding your force to his own body momentum to shift him off balance.

• *Transitional flow.* The purpose of learning the art of transitional flow is to enable you to counterattack any intentions of your adversary by fluidly moving from one technqiue to another. Watching a polished technician change techniques is an impressive experience. He moves like a dancer instead of a brawler. He is relaxed, confident, calm, quick, and mobile. His change of countertechniques is dependent on what his attacker does. Normally the first transitional change is sufficient to subdue the opponent. If necessary, he moves into a second transitional change.

Before you can do this however, you must be able to apply each individual technique proficiently. You must be able to focus efficiently, stick to your opponent, and distract your opponent's concentration effectively. The transitional flow is the most advanced art of the entire system. By the time you begin to develop the ability to apply this principle, you should be able to read your attacker's intentions, through your fingers,

palms, forearms, upper arms, and shoulders. In applying most finger and wrist locks, your ring finger or your pinky are the most sensitive parts of contact. Grip firmly but do not tighten your grip. Otherwise your opponent will be able to sense your intentions. This is why in the application of any locks it is not necessary to go into a fighting stance. It takes so little effort to create pain. Relax, stand straight, and prepare to be mobile. This is the time you do not need stability.

Mastering transitional changes enables you to constantly flow from one technique to another and still maintain total control. By cultivating a sensitivity to your opponent's slightest movement, you will be able to react spontaneously in unforeseen situations especially when you meet resistance to your original technique.

The principles of transitional changes are as follows:

- Exert continual pain during transitions. This will not only deter retaliation, but by increasing the pain as needed, discourage any escape attempt which must be anticipated since your opponent is bound to sense that the transition is his best opportunity to escape.
- Create maximum pain without dislocating the joint. This will show the attacker that you can injure him if necessary just by adding a little more pressure. This will cause him to fear you.
- Mobility is needed during transitions rather than stability.

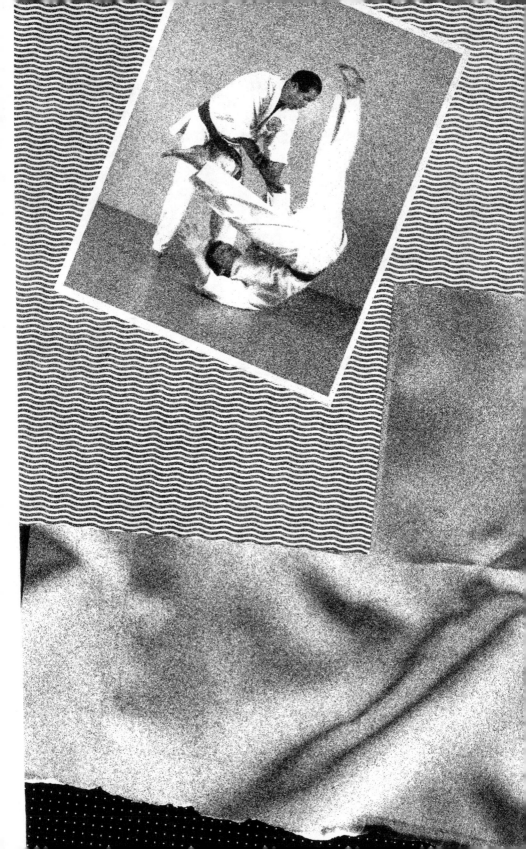

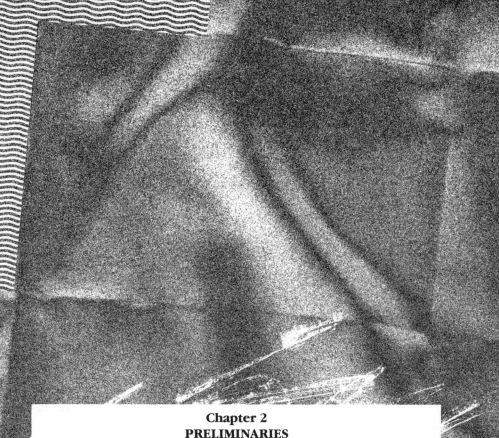

Chapter 2
PRELIMINARIES

Before starting to practice jujitsu techniques, certain skills must be learned to insure safety and to perform more effectively. These are: falling, specific key movements, and the art of resuscitation.

It is natural to fear taking a fall, but the following method will help the new student overcome this fear from the very beginning so that it is not accentuated by his anticipation of the experience. This method will allow the new student to safely take a fall after only a few minutes of instruction. The new student learns the proper way of slapping the mat, the correct angle of the slap, and the correct positioning of the body and legs when landing. This is the first step, and then the student goes on to the routine exercises and breakfalls.

Slapping correctly cushions the fall and absorbs the shock. Reaching for the mat or slapping at the incorrect angle may cause strain or dislocation of the joints. To develop the correct form, the side-to-side exercise is a must because it trains the coordination of the body, hands, feet, and legs. The entire body should be relaxed and the hands tighten only upon impact with the mat, like cracking a whip. Tucking in your chin while falling will become natural after many hours of practice.

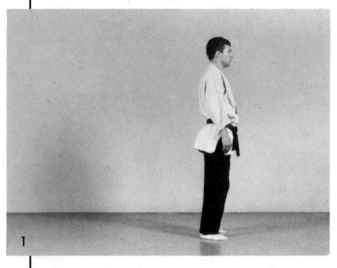

Backward Fall

(1) Stand with your hands at your sides. (2&3) Squat down and (4&5) roll onto your back. As you roll onto your upper back, slap the

mat with your arms extended 45 degrees from your sides, and exhale simultaneously. Keep your chin tucked into your chest.

Forward Shoulder Roll

(1&2) Step forward with your left foot. (3&4) Use your right arm for support. Turn your head to the right, and roll across your left arm, (5) across your back, and land

3

on your right side, making a good 45-degree angle slap with your right arm. Exhale as you slap. Practice this on both sides.

4

5

1

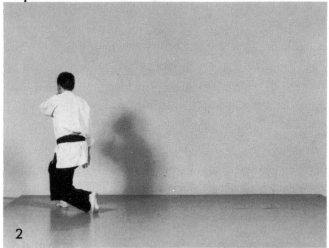

2

Backward Shoulder Roll

(1&2) Step back with your left foot, and squat down. Keep your knees close to your chest as you (3-5) roll over your right shoulder.

3

Avoid hitting your head by using your left hand to guide you. (6) Land on balance, ready to stand up.

33

1

Side to Side

(1) Begin with your left side on the mat. (2) Flip your body by scissoring your legs in the air, and (3) land on your right side, slapping with

2

3

your right arm. (4&5) Flip your body back to the left side and slap with your left arm. Repeat several times.

4

5

1

Exercise Used to Learn Proper Landing

To practice proper landing in falling, use your partner for support. (1) Have your partner hold your sleeve with both hands, and you hold onto his lapel with your right hand. (2&3) Swing your

2

legs up and forward. (4) Fall on your left side so that your hand and leg land at the same time. Keep your chin tucked to your chest, and exhale as you land.

3

4

1

2

Exercise Used to Learn Free Falls

(1) To fall from any forward throw, you must tuck your head and be able to land on your side. (2&3) Have your partner guide your head so

you do not hit it on the mat. (4) Land on your left side with a good slap of the arm. Exhale when you land.

It is vitally important to learn the key movements that are used in the application of joint locks and in the art of choking. These key movement exercises are necessary for developing fluidity in applying the small-circle techniques. First, by practicing proper entry, you will eliminate wasteful entry time. Then, by learning proper methods of application you

Basic Wrist Extension Exercise

(1-4) The basic wrist extension utilizes a simultaneous pull/push action. Pull with your little finger first then push with your thumbs, and

will eliminate the need to use power. It is natural to resort to using power, but in doing so you will telegraph your actions, and the opponent will react before you can set the hold. On the other hand, if you loosen up with these exercises, you will gain quickness.

follow with the others. At the same time, extend your forearms to add extra power to the movement.

**Wrist Extension Exercise
With Rotational Twist**

(1-5) Perform the basic wrist
extension, but this time add

a rotational twist, similar to turning a doorknob.

Wrist Extension Exercise Using Sleeves

(1&2) Fold your arms, and grab the insides of your sleeves with palms down. Then, with both wrists touching, apply the basic wrist extension movement.

Outward Wrist Stretch

This exercise will increase the flexibility needed for the bent elbow wrist lock. Turn your right hand so that the palm faces to the right, the little finger side is up, and the thumb side is down. Grab the back of your right hand with your left hand, and apply pressure by pressing your hands together, and pulling them back toward your sternum.

Inward Wrist Stretch

(1-3) Place one palm on the back of the other hand with your thumb around the wrist. Flex your wrist by pushing down on the knuckles, and bring your elbows toward the center. This will increase flexibility for all wrist-locking exercises.

Thumb Wrist Entry Exercise for Arm Bars

(1-3) Practice sliding your thumb and crook of the wrist around your own forearm to get the feel of the entry for arm bars. Avoid making a wide movement. Keep your circle small, and keep the crook of the wrist in constant contact with the forearm.

47

Thumb Wrist Entry Exercise for Arm Locks

(1) Have your partner strike with one arm. After blocking, (2&3) enter the lock by wrapping your thumb, crook of the wrist and forearm

48

tightly around the opponent's arm in a tight circle. (4) Slide your arm and do not lose contact.

3

4

Thumb Wrist Entry Exercise for Leg Bars

(1-3) Slide your thumb and crook of the wrist in a tight circle around the upper Achilles tendon and do not lose contact. Use your other hand to reinforce the hold.

1

Thumb Wrist Entry Exercise for Chokes

(1) Standing behind your partner, enter the chokehold from the side of his neck making contact with your thumb and crook of the wrist. (2) Slide without losing contact from the side of the neck to the front, positioning the thumb side of your wrist at the base of the windpipe. (3) Using your other hand to anchor your hold, tighten and simultaneously twist your choking wrist in a small circle to further press the wrist into the windpipe. Perform this movement carefully in practice.

2

3

Pivoting Exercise

Practice this exercise to learn how to face off at different angles in the ready position. (1) In the ready position, face left with your left foot in the lead. (2) Pivot on both feet 180 degrees to the right. (3) Pivot on your right foot by swinging your left foot 90 degrees behind you to face forward. (4) Pivot on both feet 180 degrees to the left. (5) Pivot on your left foot by swinging your right foot 135 degrees behind you. (6) Step forward with your right foot. (7) Pivot on your right foot by swinging your left foot 180 degrees behind you.

1

4

5

Reviving unconscious victims is a common sight. All jujitsu teachers know these revival techniques. There are variations but these are the most commonly used techniques for reviving victims who have been either choked out, knocked out, or taken a hard fall.

Knee on the Back Resuscitation

This type of resuscitation is commonly used at judo contests. (1) Reach under the victim's body while he is lying on his back, and (2) sit him up, placing your right knee between his shoulder blades. (3) Place both your hands below his breast. (4) Pull with your hands upward as you push forward with your knee. Hold for a second or two, then (5) push his breast downward as you straighten your knee. (6&7) Repeat the procedure.

5

Resuscitation From Groin Strike: Method One

(1) Place the victim in a sitting position, and hold him under both arms. (2) Lift him a few inches off the mat, and (3) drop him to the mat. Repeat this several times.

Resuscitation From Groin Strike: Method Two

Another variation is to use the sole of your foot to (1&2) strike just above the tail bone to bring the testicles back to their original positions in case they may have been pushed up to the pelvis.

Resuscitation From Groin Strike:
Method Three

(1) If the victim is on his back, raise his foot, and (2&3) use a hammerfist strike on the sole of his foot. Repeat this several times until he feels relieved.

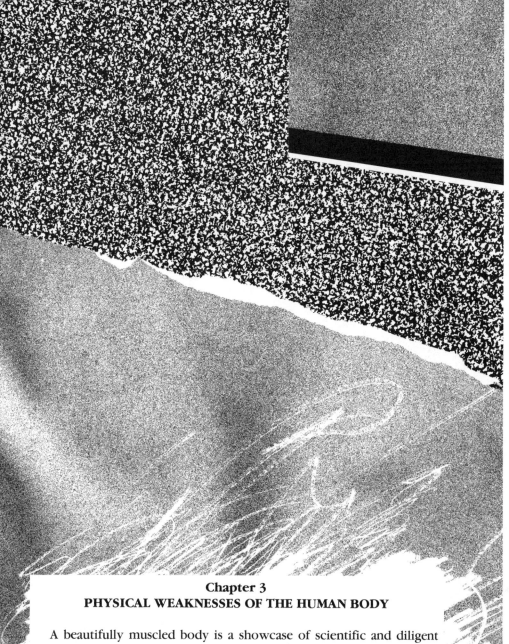

Chapter 3
PHYSICAL WEAKNESSES OF THE HUMAN BODY

A beautifully muscled body is a showcase of scientific and diligent training, but no matter how muscular a person is, his body has many built-in physical weaknesses and vulnerable areas that can be attacked to weaken him. Attacking these weak areas can cause unconsciousness, dislocations, permanent injuries, and in some cases, even death. In the techniques of small-circle jujitsu, more emphasis is put on attacking the tendons than on attacking the nerves.

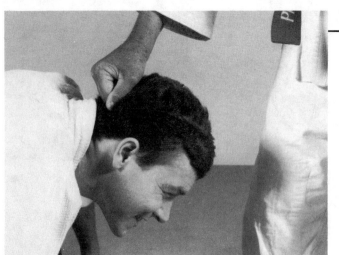

Hair

Pulling the hair can be a very painful, but effective, means of control. Pressing down with the foreknuckles enhances the effectiveness of the technique.

Chin

The best way to attack the chin is with a forceful strike, either with a fist or with the heel of the palm.

Jaw

Like the chin, the jaw is most vulnerable to a forceful strike with either fist or palm heel.

Nose

The nose is the most vulnerable target. Almost any kind of strike will break the nose.

Temple

A hard enough strike to the temple can be a killing blow. It shocks the brain and usually results in unconsciousness.

Ears

Cupping both ears hard can stun the assailant temporarily for a follow-up or even put an end to the confrontation.

Collarbone

Any kind of hand strike can very easily break the collarbone.

Windpipe

Choking techniques all depend on placing enough pressure on the windpipe to cut off breathing.

Lips

The lips can be attacked by hooking your fingers in the corners of the assailant's mouth and stretching them apart.

Floating Ribs

The floating ribs are best attacked with a punch or a palm heel strike.

Solar Plexus

Even a light strike to the solar plexus can temporarily paralyze the diaphram and severely inhibit breathing. Any striking technique with the hands, feet, or elbows will work.

Sternum

A kunckle strike to the sternum can be extremely painful to the assailant. It is a readily available target that can be struck as a distraction, or even as a primary target.

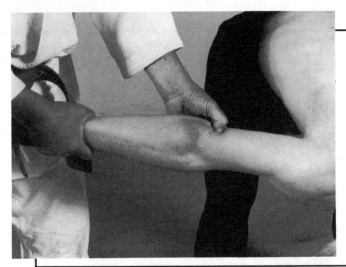

Crazy Bone

The best way of attacking the crazy bone is by applying pressure with the tip of your thumb.

Tricep

When sideshifting a blow to the outside, the tricep muscle becomes an available target.

Bicep

Striking the bicep can temporarily incapacitate that muscle. It is best attacked when countering or blocking an attempted blow by sideshifting to the inside.

Radial Bone

The radial bone is best attacked by applying pressure with the foreknuckles.

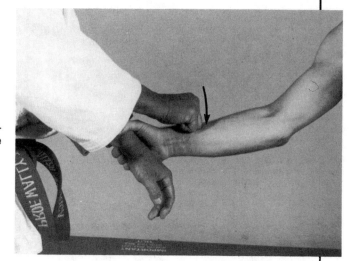

Back of Hand

The back of the hand can be attacked with a punch, or by raking the foreknuckles across the tendons.

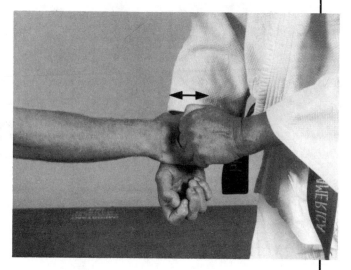

Front of the Knee

Injuring the knee from the front requires very little pressure.

Side of the Knee

Attacking the side of the knee is also best accomplished by kicking.

Shin

The shinbone is a very vulnerable target. It can be broken with a hard enough kick, and it is not easy to protect.

Calf

A kick to the calf is an excellent technique for momentarily paralyzing that muscle.

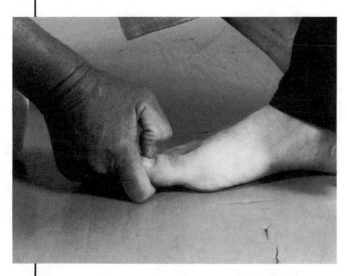

Big Toe

The big toe can be attacked by applying sharp pressure with your thumb on the cuticle of the toe.

Instep

The instep, though often used as an offensive weapon, is actually a vulnerable spot. A simple knuckle strike can easily inflict injury to that area.

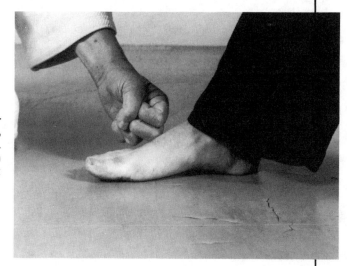

Achilles Tendon

Pressuring the Achilles tendon can be a very effective submission technique.

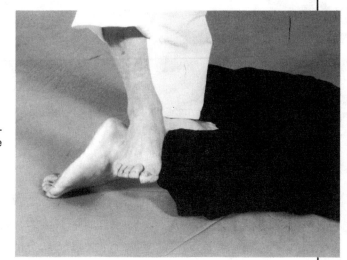

Chapter 4
SMALL-CIRCLE JUJITSU TECHNIQUES

Wrist locks are about the most common techniques among the various martial arts. Since an attacker usually attacks with his hands, the techniques for fighting or warding off the attacker's hands would naturally occur early in the development of any self-defense system. The most popular of these is probably the wrist lock throw which is known as *kote gaeshi* in aikido, and *katate tori* in kodenkan jujitsu.

Knowing when to apply the technique is as important as knowing how. The proper moment to begin application is when the assailant reaches toward you. In general, this is done by sliding your hand along his forearm toward his wrist, and when feeling the base of his hand, near the pulse below the thumb, or below the little finger, you set the hold. In the case of the opponent attempting a choke, you should apply the wrist lock with simultaneous distraction such as poking his eyes, or driving your knuckles into his sternum, or kicking his shin, to make him lose concentration on his hands and give you the split second you need to apply the technique.

When applying joint locks, a skilled technician uses minimal strength to subdue an assailant while the beginner or poorly trained technician will tend to use an unnecessary amount of force. Using a minimum of force is important because joint locks can be extremely damaging and you do not want to go beyond what is necessary to subdue and restrain your assailant. There is also a corresponding loss of sensitivity to your opponent's movements as you tighten your grip. So, grip firmly but do not tighten your sinews, and do not go into a low stance for more power. Stability and power are not necessary. Mobility is what is needed.

In practice remember also that some people are born with an ability to withstand a lot of pain. Because of this, you may mistakenly exert the full force before the student feels compelled to submit. This can cause serious injury, so always apply pressure slowly. When you feel that the hold is tight, stop. Some victims will feel little or no pain during the hold, and yet, a dislocation may have occurred. A renowned karate teacher once dislocated his partner's wrist in this way. Though his partner did not feel a dislocation or even any pain during the hold, a short time later, he had to be taken to the hospital.

When attacked, there are times when you must hurt your attacker to the point of painful dislocation. If this must be done to save yourself, do not hesitate. Joint locks will render the attacker helpless unless he is under the influence of drugs or liquor which makes him less sensitive to pain or injury.

Basic Wrist Lock

(1) As your attacker reaches toward you, slide your parallel hand along his forearm toward his wrist, and when you feel the base of his hand, near the pulse, below the thumb, (2) set your grip. Plant the tip of your thumb firmly between the last two knuckles of the back of his hand. Wrap your other fingers around the inside of his hand, turn his wrist so his palm faces him, and apply the small-circle pressure by pushing with your thumb and pulling with your fingers.

Cross Arm Wrist Lock

(1) Place your hand over the assailant's knuckles with your thumb in the web of his hand, and your fingers over the edge of his hand. (2) Push directly downward on the knuckles.

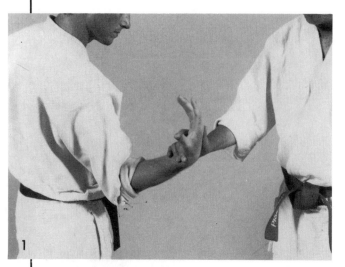

Cross Arm Wrist Lock Variation

Another variation involves (1) gripping the assailant's hand so your thumb is placed in the web between his thumb and index finger. Wrap your other fingers around the last two fingers and edge of his hand. (2) Pull with your thumb and push with your fingers as you maintain the 90-degree bend at the elbow, and push straight downward.

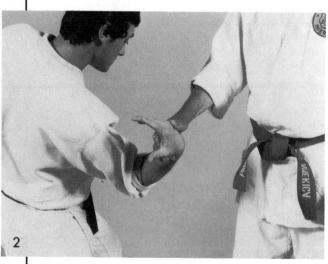

Bent Elbow Wrist Lock

(1) As the assailant reaches toward you, reach over his hand with your cross hand so your palm covers the back of his hand. (2) Wrap your fingers around the edge of his hand, and plant the tip of your thumb in the web between his thumb and index finger. (3) Turn his hand so his little finger is on top and his palm is facing to the right. Then apply the small circle by pulling with your fingers and pressing forward with your thumb. Apply additional pressure by pushing his hand forward, and with your free hand, pressing down on his forearm to bend his elbow.

Extended Wrist Lock

(1) Enter this technique just like the bent elbow wrist lock, but the opponent counters by rotating his elbow up and keeping it straight. (2) Reinforce your hold by gripping with your free hand as well. Both your thumbs should be together on the knuckles in the middle of the back of his hand. Wrap your other fingers around the inside of his palm and wrist. (3) Push with your thumbs and pull with your fingers, forcing his palm toward his centerline.

2

3

1

Goose Neck Hold

This is a parallel arm technique. (1) Grab your opponent's right wrist with your right hand. (2) Pull him off balance as you step behind him. (3) Bring your left arm underneath his right arm and cover the back of his knuckles with your left palm. At this point his elbow

2

3

and wrist should be naturally bent, and the elbow anchored between your ribs and inner bicep just underneath your armpit. (4) Direct your pressure slowly to press his knuckles into his forearm using two-way circular action.

4

Reverse Goose Neck Hold

From the extended wrist lock, you can (1) shift your grip by planting your thumb in the web between the opponent's thumb and index finger. Wrap your fingers around the edge of his palm, and (2&3) apply pressure against the back of his knuckles by pulling in with your fingers and pressing forward with your thumb toward his centerline. At the same time, place the web of your other hand just above his elbow at the tricep tendon, and press downward.

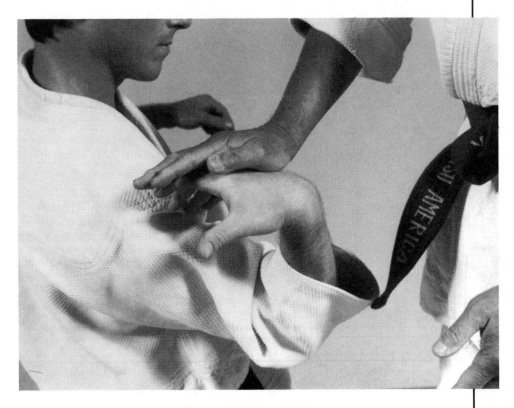

Palm Press Wrist Lock

The wrist lock can also be applied with a pressing motion. It is a cross arm technique. Place your hand on the back of the assailant's hand so that your fingers and thumb are on top of his. Press straight down on the back of his knuckles, maintaining the 90-degree bend at the elbow. The assailant will either be taken to the ground or receive an injured wrist.

83

Underhand Wrist Lock

This is a cross arm technique. From a double wrist grab, (1&2) grab the thumb of your opponent with all your fingers. (3) Place your own thumb between the last

two knuckles of the opponent's. (4) Push with your thumb as you pull with your fingers to produce the twisting action focused toward his elbow.

Vertical Wrist Lock

This technique is similar to aikido's *sankyo*, but the point of focus here is on the opponent's little finger. This is a parallel arm technique. (1) Wrap your fingers around the back of the opponent's hand, and grab his little finger. Cross your thumb over his thumb knuckle at a right angle. (2) Push with your thumb and pull with your fingers in a counterclockwise direction into the opponent's centerline. (3) A properly applied lock will force the opponent up on his toes in an unbalanced position, and in extreme pain. Practice with caution.

Chicken Wing

This technique is similar to the goose neck hold except the opponent's wrist is bent upward instead of downward. (1-3) Walk behind your opponent and grab his thumb so your fingers grip the pad of his thumb, and your thumb hooks in the web between his thumb and index finger. Bend down slightly and anchor the elbow on your ribs. (4&5) Apply pressure across the opponent's knuckles by pressing them toward his forearm. Apply the small-circle movement of pushing with your thumb and pulling with your fingers. This will produce great pain and will tend to force the opponent up on his toes.

3

5

Finger locks are very effective and can be applied with very little effort. One of my students, a 110-pound girl, was able to control and subdue a man twice her size with a two-finger hold. Another female student with only one lesson subdued a mugger a few hours after the lesson using a one-finger hold.

At a demonstration during one of my tours to New Zealand, I brought a larger man to the mat on his stomach with a one-finger hold. I then asked a little boy to apply the pressure on him with a one-finger hold. The child was cautioned to do it slowly. Much to the spectators' surprise, the victim meekly surrendered. The child was five years old, yet possessed sufficient power to subdue a large man.

1

Index Finger Lock

(1) As your assailant points his finger toward your face, (2) grab his finger with your left hand, so that your little finger wraps around the base of his knuckle. (3) Apply the small-circle method

2

by pushing forward on the tip of his finger while pulling in with your last two fingers. (4&5) You can take your assailant to the ground and pin him with this lock.

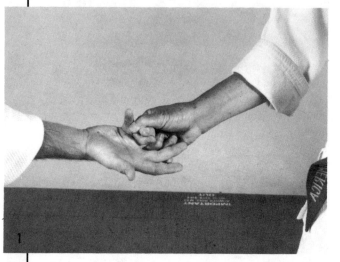

Ring Finger Lock

(1&2) To set the ring finger lock, wrap your index finger around your opponent's ring finger, and use your thumb to press down on the end of his finger as you pull up with your index finger. Another way to pressure the ring finger is to use the tip of your thumb to press down on the cuticle. A third way is to apply thumb pressure from the side of the finger.

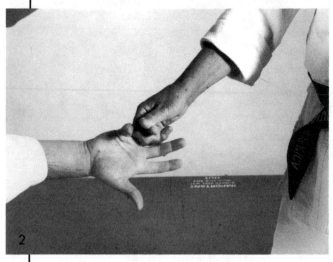

Two Finger Lock

(1) Grab the opponent's last two fingers. Turn his hand palm up and apply pressure by rotating your wrist. To increase the effectiveness of this lock, (2) use your index finger as a bar and press it into the back of his knuckles as you pull the fingertips back toward his forearm.

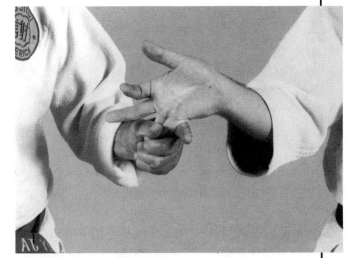

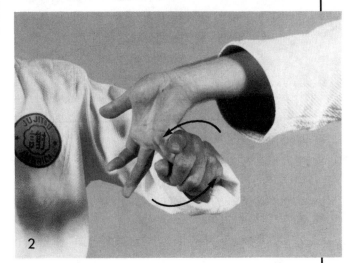

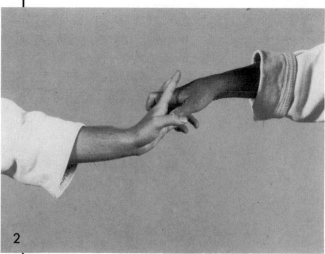

1

Interlocking Fingers

(1) Lace your fingers in your opponent's. (2) Cross your fingers over his, and (3) turn his palm upward. (4) Apply

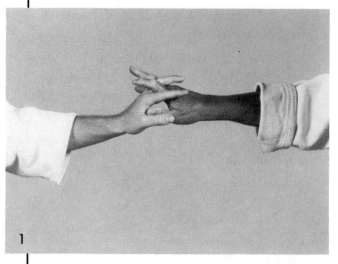

2

pressure by forcing his fingers back toward his forearm to keep him off balance.

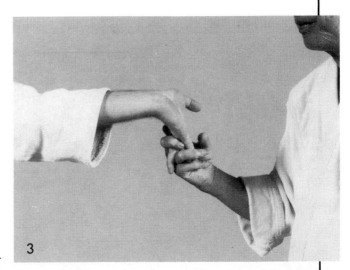

3

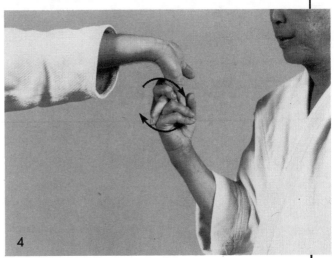

4

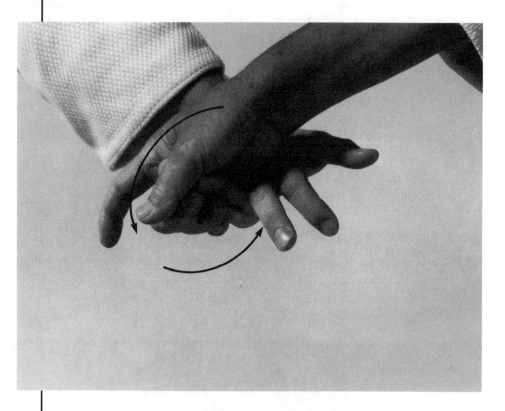

Reverse Two Finger Lock

Grab the opponent's hand so the edge of your palm presses against the backs of his knuckles and your fingers wrap around his last two fingers. Apply pressure by pulling back on his fingertips toward his forearm, and press down on his knuckles with the edge of your hand.

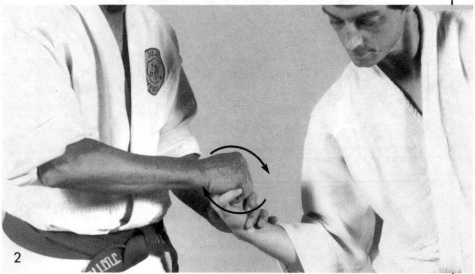

Compress Fingers Lock

(1) Cover the opponent's fingers with the palm of your own hand so that your fingertips push directly down on the opponent's fingertips. (2) Push in with your own palm as you push down with your fingertips. Properly applied, the pain will be intense.

Pistol Grip

This is a parallel arm technique. (1) Approach from the side. (2) Grasp the opponent's thumb with all your fingers with your thumb around his wrist. (3) Apply pressure by pulling his thumb toward his forearm. Practice slowly because this hold can be very painful. This hold may be used to bring the opponent up off the ground onto his feet.

2

3

After extensive research on the arm bar and arm lock application, I've become a strong believer in attacking the tricep tendon during the application of these holds. The target area of Kodokan judo and many traditional styles of jujitsu emphasize applying pressure against the elbow joint. The only time I advise putting pressure against the elbow joint or

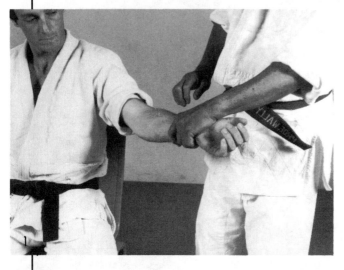

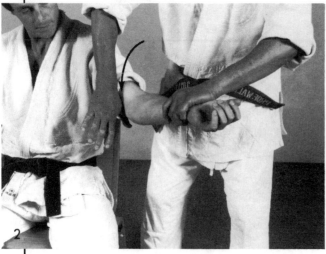

Regular Arm Bar

(1&2) Circle your right hand tightly around the opponent's extended arm just above his elbow. This is the same area of the tricep tendon. (3) Keep his arm extended with your left hand, and press down slowly but with increasing pressure. (4)

knee joint is when striking with a kick or striking with the palm, fist, or forearm. For control, I emphasize putting pressure on the tricep tendon. This renders the victim helpless and dislocation of the joints can be applied at any time at the defender's discretion.

By grabbing your own lapel, you can anchor the lock and apply the small-circle wrist extension so your radial bone is driven into the sensitive tricep tendon. Be very careful. Additional pressure will break this joint.

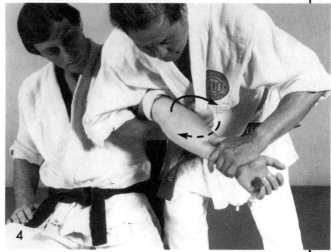

1

2

Reverse Elbow on Elbow Arm Bar

As the assailant (1&2) jabs at you, fade back, and grab his right wrist with your left hand. (3) Use your right hand to keep the assailant's wrist turned so his little finger is on top. Anchor his wrist against your chest, and (4) apply downward pressure with your elbow on his tricep tendon, and upward pressure on his forearm. This will drive him to one knee and keep him there with a dislocated elbow.

1

2

Reverse Arm Bar Using Armpit

A variation of the reverse arm bar is to use your armpit to apply the pressure on the tricep tendon. (1&2) Fade back and grab the assailant's wrist as he jabs at you. (3) Using both your hands, pull him in the direction of his punch to keep him off balance. Bring your left arm over his right arm with his tricep tendon under your armpit. Apply downward pressure as you pull up with your hands. This is a simultaneous push/pull action. Dropping your own body to the ground suddenly will dislocate the joint.

3

Reverse Arm Bar Using Palm Strike to Elbow

(1&2) Quickly grab the assailant's left arm just above his elbow with your right hand. This is the tricep tendon area. (3) Push with your right hand toward the center of his body as you grab his extended hand with your left hand. Keep his palm turned up as you apply a downward palm strike with your right hand. To apply the small-circle push/pull action, push with your right hand and pull with your left.

103

Reverse Arm Bar Using Knuckle Drive Into Tricep Tendon

(1) Grab the assailant at the tricep tendon, just above the elbow. (2) As you pull him off balance toward you with your left hand, cup your palm directly over the elbow, and (3) roll your fore-knuckles into the tricep ten-

3

don. (4) Continue to pull back and down with your left hand as you apply pressure on the tendon with your knuckles. (5) This will bring him flat on his stomach and under control.

4

5

Reverse Arm Bar Using Knuckle Rub on Tendon

(1) Apply the arm bar, and (2) roll your foreknuckles into the tricep tendon, then (3) rake your knuckles across the tendon, applying downward pressure, and rubbing vigorously from side to side.

2

3

Reverse Arm Bar Using Foot Stomp

(1) After you have taken the assailant to the ground with the reverse arm bar, (2) stretch his arm at a right angle to his body so that his wrist rests on your left instep. (3) Use your right foot to slowly apply pressure on the tricep tendon by stepping down on it slowly. This will control the assailant. If you stomp on the tricep tendon with your right foot, you will inflict severe damage to the joint.

Eviction Technique Head Control

(1) Grab the assailant's left wrist with your own left hand, and (2) move to his outside. Snake your right arm under his left arm at the tricep tendon, and (3) place your palm on the back of his neck. This will anchor your lock. Apply slow and steady downward pressure with your left hand, keeping his palm turned up. This will generate pain on the tricep tendon and cause the person to stand up.

Eviction Technique Using Lapel Grip

Another variation of the arm bar is to anchor the lock by (1) grabbing high on the lapel rather than behind the neck. (2) Apply the small-circle wrist extension with your right hand, pushing away from your body. (3) Slow and steady downward pressure with your left hand will generate pain on the tricep tendon with your forearm. This will force him to his feet. Or, you may trap his forearm behind your back.

2

3

2

3

2

3

Hammer Lock

(1) As you parry the opponent's arm with your parallel hand, grab the back of his elbow with the other and (2) pull it toward you so it bends. Then (3) snake your parallel arm under the opponent's arm, planting the edge of your hand into the crook of his elbow. (4) Pull in his arm to cradle the forearm against your body with his wrist anchored over the inside of your own elbow. Apply pressure by raising your elbow and pushing down and toward your own centerline with your hand. This will force him off balance and he will move away from you. (5) You can pull him back by pressing on his shoulder nerve, (6) pulling his hair, or (7-9) sliding your free hand around his windpipe.

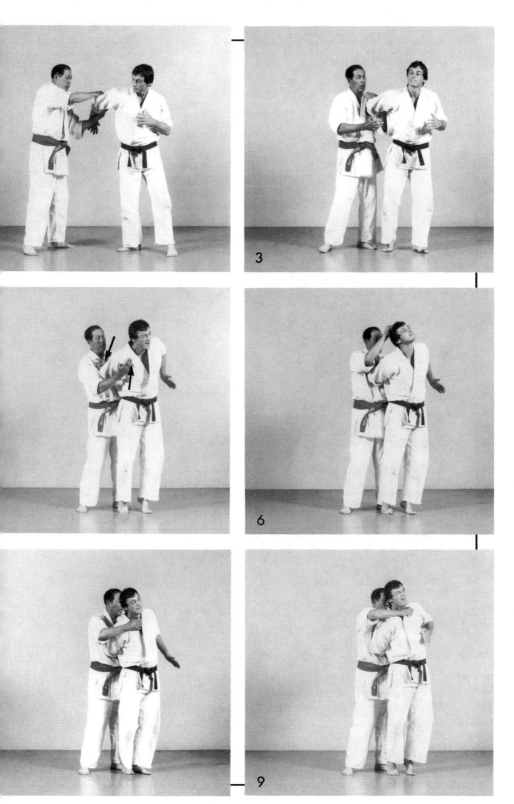

3

6

9

The leg techniques are usually applied on the Achilles tendon, calves, toes, and knees. Attacking the Achilles tendon produces unbearable pain, comparable to the pain suffered from an attack on the tendon of the tricep.

The toe hold or foot hold applied with the two-way wrist action are

Takedown

(1&2) Deflect the assailant's left jab with your right hand. (3) Drop to your left knee, and drive your left shoulder

ample proof that the small-circle techniques are much superior to the old one-way action. The two-way action of the small-circle techniques brings on pain with very little effort.

into his knee as you pull back on his ankle with both hands. (4) This will take him to the ground.

Leg Bar

(1) Move to the assailant's outside as you deflect his right jab with your left palm. (2&3) Drop low to your right knee, and plant your right forearm just above his right knee. Grab his ankle with your left hand, and (4) press

4

forward with your right forearm to take him down. (5&6) Wrap your right arm tightly around the assailant's lower calf, and apply the small-circle wrist extension to drive your radial bone into his Achilles tendon.

5

6

One Leg Step Over

(1-5) Using the same entry to bring down the opponent use the leg bar to capture his leg. Then, (6) keeping pressure on his Achilles tendon, step over his body with your left leg. This will turn him on his stomach. (7) Plant your right foot between his legs close to his groin. (8) Apply pressure with your left hand by pushing forward on his toes.

5

8

Leg Lock

(1-6) From the one leg step over, you can apply the leg lock. (7) Use your right shin to attack the Achilles tendon by dropping to your knees with your right shin across the back of the opponent's knee joint, and apply pressure by pushing forward on his toes. (8) Or, you may instead place his instep against your sternum, and apply pressure by pressing forward with your body.

5

8

Leg Screw Combination

This is a combination of the leg screw followed by a leg lock, followed by the reverse Indian death lock. (1&2) Execute the takedown. (3) Grab the assailant's right foot. (4) Place your right foot at his hip, and his left foot on your lap. Push downward with your elbow to create a painful leg screw. (5) The assailant will bring his left foot up to resist. (6) Grab his right foot and pull it forward so his right foot is trapped inside the natural bend of his left knee joint. (7) Grab his left foot and place it at the back of your thigh and push forward with your right knee to create a painful leg lock. (8) Twist to your left to turn the assailant on his stomach. (9&10) Use the inside of your own right knee to apply forward pressure against the assailant's foot, thus creating the reverse Indian death lock.

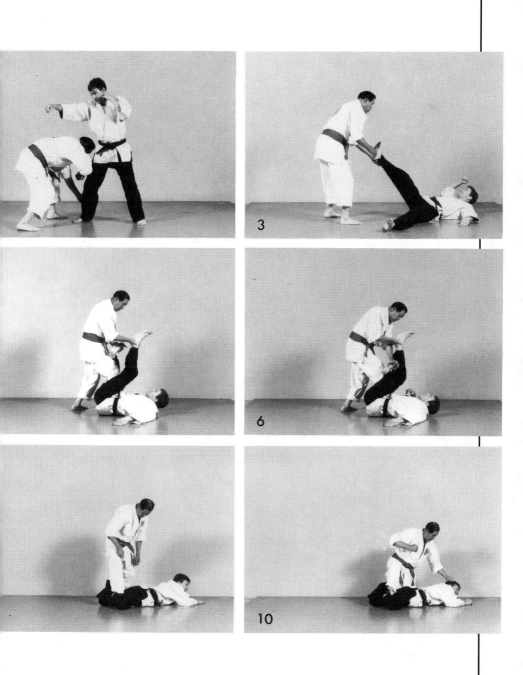

Hip Throw

(1&2) Your assailant punches at your head with a left-right combination. Block these with forearm strikes to his biceps. Pull him off balance with your left arm, and (3) place your right arm around his waist as you step across in front of him with your right foot. (4) Pivot counterclockwise on the

ball of your right foot to face the same direction as your assailant. Squat low so your hips are lower than his, and to the outside. (5) Pull forward with your left hand, and quickly straighten your legs to throw him over your hip. (6) Your assailant will land in front of you on his left side.

1

Wrist Lock Throw

(1) As the attacker reaches for you, apply the one hand seizure grip from the side with your free hand. (2&3) Push the attacker's wrist toward your waist. This movement will unbalance him to his right, and cause great pain if done quickly. It will also tear the ligaments, and possibly dislocate the wrist. Apply pressure slowly and smoothly in practice to allow your partner to take the fall without injury.

2

3

Arm Bar Throw

(1) You are grabbed on the outside of both wrists. Point your fingers straight up, and (2) grab the inside of your assailant's wrists. (3) Cross his left arm under his right arm, and step across with your right foot. (4) Pivot counterclockwise under his armpit. (5) Step back with your left foot. (6&7) Push with your left hand as you pull with your right. This will throw him to the ground or break his right elbow.

5

Arm Bar Throw Variation

(1) Your assailant tries to reach around your head with his left arm. (2&3) Wrap your right arm over his upper left arm, pinning it behind your neck, and pull his right arm with your left hand. Step in and pivot on the ball of your right foot as you squat low. (4&5) Pull with your left arm as you snap your legs straight. This will throw the assailant on his left side.

1

3

5

Arm Lock Throw

(1) As your assailant attempts a two-handed wrist grab on your right wrist, (2) rotate your right palm up in a clockwise direction, and grab the assailant's right wrist. (3) With your left hand, grab his left wrist, and (4) lock his right elbow inside his left elbow. (5) Pivot counterclockwise on your left foot and push with your left hand as you pull with your right hand. This (6&7) will throw him or break his right elbow.

5

Double Sleeve Throw

(1) Your assailant applies a two-handed front choke. (2&3) Push up on his left elbow with your right palm, and pull forward on his sleeve with your left hand.

(4) Step in with your right foot, squat low, and then (5) straighten your legs sharply as you pull him forward and throw him over your hip. (6) He will land on his back.

Shoulder Throw

(1) Your assailant attempts a two-handed front choke. Grab his right arm with your left hand. (2) Swing your right arm over his left elbow, and (3) shoot it down and across to the other side. Place the inside of your right elbow under his right arm-

4

pit, and (4) lift as you step in and pivot on the ball of your right foot. Be sure to squat low. (5) Pull forward with your arm. Snap your legs straight and throw him over your shoulder so the assailant (6) lands on his left side.

5

6

Over-the-Shoulder Throw

(1&2) Block your assailant's right punch with your left forearm. (3) Step in deeply with your right leg as you pull his left arm so his waist

is loaded onto your shoulder. (4&5) Stand up and toss him over your left shoulder. (6) He will land on his left side.

137

Winding Throw

(1) Your assailant attempts to apply a full nelson. (2) Straighten your neck, raise your right arm, and anchor his right arm tightly to your right armpit. (3) Drop low to

3

your right knee and (4) throw your assailant over your right shoulder. (5) You will land on top of your assailant, ready to apply a submission.

4

5

Hook Foot Sweep

(1&2) From your own right lead, parry the assailant's left jab. (3) Push his left elbow toward his center to off balance him. (4) Slide in and plant your right ankle be-

4

hind his left heel. (5) Sweep your ankle forward and pull your right arm back. (6) This will throw your assailant flat on his back.

5

6

Front Locking Knee Throw

(1) From a two handed reach by your assailant, grab inside his arms and pull him off balance. (2) Step in with your right foot, and (3) plant the inside of your instep be-

hind his right ankle. (4) Press forward with your right knee so the assailant's leg is locked straight. This action will (5) take the assailant down on his back.

1

Side Locking Knee Throw

(1) Your assailant applies a rear bear hug. (2&3) Plant your right ankle behind his right ankle. (4) Press side-

2

3

ward with your right knee to (5) take the assailant down on his back.

4

5

Sitting Leg Lock Throw

(1) As your opponent applies a rear bear hug, (2&3) hook your right foot behind his right ankle. (4&5) Sit back on his knee as you sweep his

146

right foot forward and up. This is a dangerous technique, so lower your weight slowly when you sit back.

Rear Reaping Throw

(1&2) Beat your assailant's attempted punch by striking his left shoulder with your right palm. Then, (3&4) slide in and hook your right knee joint around the inside of

the assailant's left knee. (5) Pull back with your right leg as you push with your right hand. This will (6) take him down on his back.

1

2

Outside Reaping Throw

(1&2) Block your assailant's punch with your left forearm. (3) Pull down on his right arm with your left hand, and apply a right palm under his chin. This will unbalance him, and allow you

3

to move close and (4&5) sweep out his left leg with your right leg. Sweep back and up with your right leg as you push forward with your right palm. This will (6) throw him hard on his back.

Circle Throw

(1&2) As your assailant pushes you with both hands, grab under his elbows with your hands. (3) Plant your right foot directly on his stomach, and drop down on your back and

4

under the assailant as you pull him toward you. (4) When he is directly over you, quickly straighten your leg. This will (5&6) throw him head over heels so he lands on his back.

5

6

Flying Scissors

(1) From a right defensive posture, (2) parry your assailant's left jab. (3&4) Grab his left shoulder or arm and jump forward with your right leg across the front of his

hips, and (5) scissors your left leg behind both your assailant's legs. The scissoring action will take him to his back.

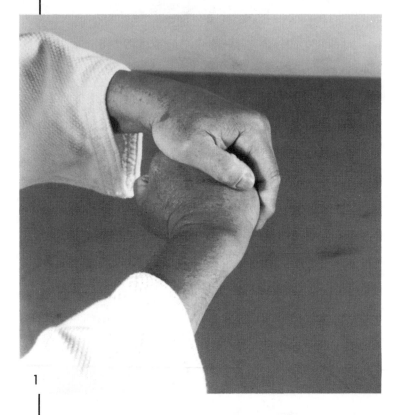

1

Using the Crook of the Wrist in Chokes

The crook of the wrist (at your radial bone) is used in the small-circle choking techniques. (1-3) Apply the wrist extension with your right hand, using your left hand as anchor. This drives the crook of your wrist into the opponent's windpipe or into the carotid artery.

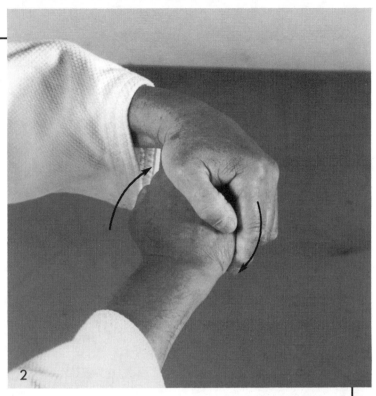

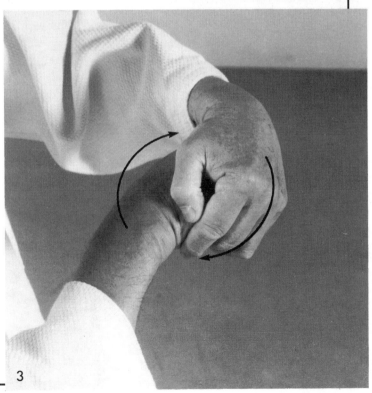

1

2

Front Naked Choke

(1&2) Slide your left hand behind the assailant's neck and pull his head forward and down. (3) Tightly wrap your right arm around his throat. Plant the crook of your wrist on the base of his windpipe, and anchor your right hand by grabbing it with your left. (4) Apply the small-circle wrist extension with your right hand so your inner wrist bone is driven into the base of the assailant's windpipe.

3

4

Rear Naked Choke

(1&2) Turn the opponent as you slip behind him and plant the crook of your wrist at the base of his windpipe. If he has a collar to grab, use that to anchor your hand. Otherwise, (3) use your left hand to grab on top of your right to reinforce the choke. (4) Step back to off balance him, and at the same time, apply the small-circle wrist extension to apply pressure on the base of the windpipe.

3

4

Naked Hands
Interlock Choke

(1) Wrap your right arm around the assailant's throat so the crook of your wrist is pressed on the base of his windpipe. (2) Plant the edge of your right hand in your left elbow joint. (3)

Place the edge of your left hand behind the assailant's neck. (4) Apply the small-circle wrist extension with both of your wrists. This will put pressure on the windpipe.

3

4

Bent Index Finger Choke

(1&2) Use your left palm to hold the opponent's head in position. (3) Place your in-

3

dex finger at the base of his windpipe. (4&5) Press in and slightly down.

4

5

Double Sleeve Choke

(1&2) Grab the assailant's left elbow with your right hand. Pull him clockwise as you move behind him. Check his left elbow with your left hand. (3) Wrap your right arm around his throat. (4) Grab the inside of your left sleeve with your right hand. (5) Place your left forearm across the back of his neck, and grab the outside of your right sleeve with your left hand. (6) Apply the small-circle wrist extension with your right hand to execute the choke.

1

4

2

3

5

6

Double Lapel Standing Choke

(1) Insert the fingers of your right hand under the right lapel of your opponent just above his clavicle and grip. (2) Cross your left hand under your right and grip the opposite lapel in the same manner. (3) Pull him close to you as you apply the small-circle wrist extension with your right wrist.

Arm Lock Choke

(1&2) As your assailant throws a right jab, parry it to the outside with your left palm. (3) Wrap your right arm around his right arm and neck. (4) Press forward with your right shoulder as you drive your wrist into the nerves on the other side of his neck, and into the carotid artery. (5) Move behind him slightly to secure the hold.

168

2

3

2

4

5

1

2

Lapel Noose Choke

(1&2) Stand over your opponent's right side. Grab inside his right lapel with the fingers of your right hand. (3) Plant your left wrist (the ulna bone) on the back of his neck. Get a strong grip with your right hand, and draw the opponent's lapel across his throat. (4) Rotate your right fist to a thumb-up position and apply the small-circle wrist extension with your right hand as you press down on the back of his neck with your left.

3

4

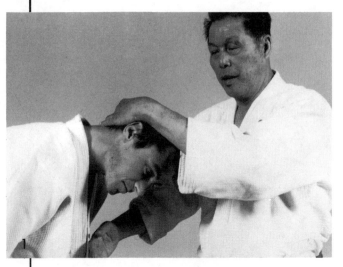

Hawaiian Choke

(1) Approach your opponent from his left side. (2) Plant the crook of your right wrist at the base of his windpipe. (3) Place your left forearm across the back of his neck,

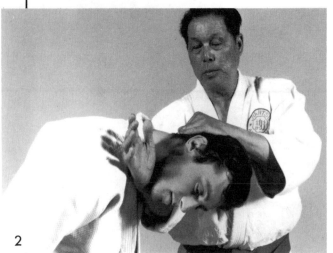

2

and interlace your fingers. (4) Tighten slowly. Push down with your left wrist as you apply the small-circle wrist extension with your right wrist.

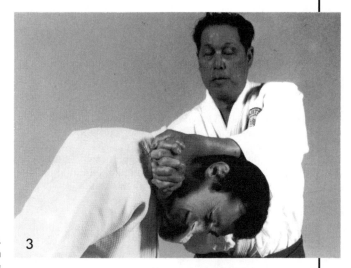

3

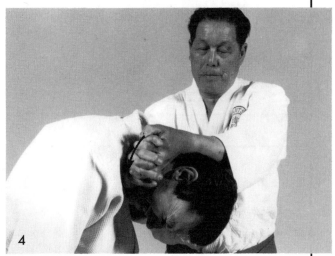

4

3

One-Wing Choke

(1&2) Push the assailant's left shoulder with your right palm. At the same time, pull his right elbow with your left hand. (3) Spin him counterclockwise so you step behind him. Grip his left lapel with your right hand, thumb on the inside. (4) Slip your left palm under his left arm and up against the back of his neck in a half nelson. (5) Apply the small-circle wrist extension with your right wrist as you snake your left hand behind his neck (palm facing out) to tighten the hold.

1

Wall Choke

You can use a wall to create a base for the assailant. (1&2) Insert your thumb inside his right lapel. Placing your outer wrist bone across the base of his windpipe (3) grab his left lapel with your left hand. Pull tightly to your left shoulder with your left hand as you apply the small-circle wrist extension with your right.

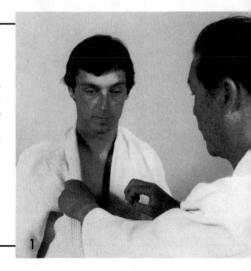

1

2

4

5

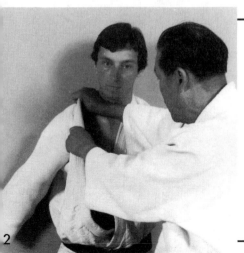

2

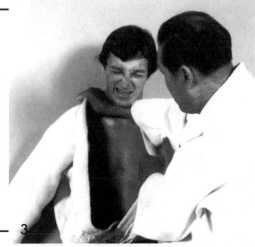

— 3

Chapter 5
SELF-DEFENSE

A mugger usually looks for someone who seems an easy prey. Trained martial artists are very aware of their own whereabouts. They are always mentally on guard entering or leaving a building, car, or home. They are aware of adverse conditions, and have in their minds several courses of action to take should they be attacked. They will decide quickly whether they should face the muggers or avoid the confrontation. To run away is not cowardice, but wisdom at times.

Muggings are done at close quarters. This is the range in which jujitsu techniques work best. In a fist attack, it's best to attack the back of the attacker's closed fist, or attack his forearms, and then the upper arms before executing locks. Use short hooks and cross blows. Attack the triceps from the outside, and the biceps from the inside. It is better to demolish the missile site than to stop the missles en route. Immobilize the arms or legs to weaken the attack. As soon as this is effective (the pain will be visible), locks and chokes will become available to you as options. It is better to fight standing than to grapple on the ground as there may be other members of the attacking party present.

Bent Arm Against Round Punch

(1&2) The assailant attempts to punch you with his right fist. Block the punch at his elbow joint with your left forearm. (3) Wrap your left arm tightly around his right elbow at the tricep tendon. (4) Plant your right

3

palm on his right shoulder. (5) Grab your own right wrist with your left hand and apply the small-circle wrist extension with your left wrist. The pain on his tricep tendon will keep him off balance and under submission.

4

5

Arm Lock Against Cross Punch

(1&2) Your assailant throws a right swing to your face. Move to his outside and hook your right wrist around his elbow joint. (3) Keep his

forearm trapped tightly to your chest and bow forward. (4&5) Bring him to the ground.

1

Reverse Arm Lock Against Straight Punch

(1) Your assailant throws a right jab. (2) Step to his outside and parry his jab to the right with your left hand. At the same time, hook your right forearm around his

2

right forearm. (3&4) Drive your left forearm into the tricep tendon of his right arm. Press down with your left forearm as you pull up with your right forearm.

Reverse Arm Bar Against Overhead Strike

(1&2) Shift left to the assailant's outside as you strike his tricep tendon with your left arm. (3) Allow his downward motion to continue as you roll your left forearm clockwise so you can (4) apply a reverse arm bar. (5&6)

Use your forearm and ulna bone to apply downward pressure on the tricep tendon. Remember to pull up with your right hand as you push down with your left forearm.

185

1

2

Shoulder and Elbow Lock Against Overhead Strike

To counter a club attack, (1&2) intercept the attack at the stem, the butt end, of the weapon. (3) Snake your right arm under the assailant's right elbow, and grip on top

3

of your own left hand. (4) Pull down with your hands as you pry up with your right elbow. This will lock the assailant's elbow and shoulder, and (5) take him down.

4

5

Arm Punches Against Jab

(1) Your assailant throws a left jab. Parry with your left and move to the outside. (2) Strike the back of his left fist with a right vertical punch. (3) Immediately attack his left forearm with a left vertical fist, and (4) follow this up

with a rapid right vertical fist to his tricep tendon. These three strikes should be thrown as a combination in one second. However, each strike is designed to paralyze the arm.

3

4

Hammerlock Against Chest Shove

(1&2) The assailant shoves you in the chest with his right hand. Fade back with your left foot. Deflect his right forearm with your left forearm circling clockwise. At the same time, use your right hand to grab the back of his elbow. (3) Pull with your right hand so his elbow bends toward you. (4) Step behind him as you plant the

3

edge of your left hand in the bend of his elbow. (5) To apply pressure, lift your elbow up as you apply the small-circle wrist extension with your left hand. To stop the assailant from bending forward to escape the pain, press your right hand back toward you on his right shoulder.

4

5

Palm Finger Press Against Chest Shove

(1&2) The assailant shoves you with his right hand. (3) Place both of your palms under his elbow. Pull his elbow outward, then toward

you so it bends naturally. (4) Press forward with your chest to apply pressure on his fingertips.

3

4

Duck Under Arm

(1) The assailant attacks with a two handed frontal choke. (2) Duck your head between the assailant's arms. (3&4) Break his grip by

3

moving your head under his arms and to the outside. The assailant's body will be vulnerable for (5) a counterattack.

4

5

1

Wedge Out With One Arm

(1) If you are unable to duck under to escape the choke, it is because the assailant has concentrated his efforts to your throat. Wedge out with one arm by (2) positioning your right arm between

2

his arms. (3&4) Step back with your left leg as you shoot your right arm upward. This will create the leverage needed to (5) break his hold. The assailant will be open for a counterattack.

Pressure on Tricep Tendon One

(1) Your assailant attacks with a two handed frontal choke. Plant the web of your hands under the tricep tendons. (2) Push up on the tendons. This will off balance him and release his grip. From here, you are in a good position to counterattack.

Pressure on Tricep Tendon Two

This technique is useful in situations where you are restricted from stepping back, such as being against a wall. As the assailant (1) attempts a two handed choke, (2) drive your fore-knuckles directly into the tricep tendons. Direct the force upward. (3) This will uproot him and send him back.

Trapped Arm Lock

(1) The assailant attacks with a two hand choke. (2&3) Pull on his right sleeve just below the elbow with your left hand, and snake your right hand over his left arm and down between his arms to break his grip. Draw him closer to you to trap his left forearm. (4) Release your grip on his sleeve. Grab the fingers of his right hand with your right hand and (5) take him to the ground by pulling his right hand down. (6) Hold him helpless on the ground by (7) planting your right knee on his tricep tendon, and apply the small-circle wrist extension as you pull his hand toward you.

5

Figure Four Arm Bar

(1) Your assailant attacks with a two handed frontal choke. (2) Extend your right arm
between his arms. (3) Wrap your right arm
around his left elbow. (4&5) Drive your right
radial bone into his tricep tendon to complete the release. Use your left hand to
assist in pressing your radial bone into his
tendon.

5

Arm Lift Throw

(1) As the assailant attempts a front choke, (2) pin his right elbow joint to your body with your left forearm, and (3) push his left elbow upward with your right hand. Continue your simul-

taneous push/pull in a counterclockwise direction as you (4) step back with your left foot. This will (5&6) take the assailant to the ground, open to a joint lock.

Reverse Arm Bar One

(1) Your assailant applies a cross lapel choke. (2) Anchor your right hand on his lower right hand while you (3&4) shoot your left forearm under his tricep tendon and grab his lapel (fingers on the inside, and thumb on the outside). (5&6) Keep your right hand anchored, and apply the small-circle wrist extension with your left hand to drive your left forearm into his tricep tendon, and drive your knuckles into his clavicle.

3

6

Reverse Arm Bar Two

(1) From a cross lapel choke, you can apply a reverse arm bar. (2) Anchor your assailant's left hand by grabbing it with your left hand. (3) Step back with your left foot as you sweep your right arm over his in a counterclockwise motion. This will allow

you to use leverage against him. (4) Apply downward pressure with your armpit on the tricep tendon as you pull up on his wrist. Remember to apply the simultaneous push/pull method slowly.

3

4

Reverse Arm Bar and Side Kick

(1) An arm over the shoulders can easily become a strong side head lock. To escape this, (2) squat low to maintain your balance, and drive your right fist or palm hard into his groin. (3) Tuck your chin toward him and in-

to your chest. Plant your left palm under his right armpit and push away to escape. (4) If he drops his arm you can apply a quick elbow wrench arm bar, or (5&6) drive a low side kick into his knee joint.

Reverse Arm Bar and Pin

(1) The assailant cups his right hand over your mouth from behind. (2) Place your right palm under his right elbow, and place your left palm across his right hand. (3) Spin counterclockwise

and duck under his arm. (4) Apply a reverse arm bar using your foreknuckles to apply pressure to the tricep tendon. (5&6) Walk backward to take him down on his stomach.

Vertical Wrist Lock

From a seated position, (1) the assailant puts his arm over your shoulders. (2) Grab his hand with your right hand, and quickly drive your left elbow back into his face. (3) While controlling his right

3

arm, slip your head out from underneath his right arm to escape, then (4&5) apply a vertical wrist lock with the wrist turned in to hold him in submission.

4

5

Wrist Lock Throw

(1) The assailant applies a rear two-hand neck choke. (2) Reach up with your right hand and grab his right thumb pad. (3&4) Spin clockwise, face your assailant, and plant your left hand on

4

the back of his right hand. (5&6) Apply the under hand wrist lock hold, and use the small-circle wrist extension with your right hand to take him down.

5

6

Against Lapel Grab One

(1) The assailant grabs your lapel with his right hand. (2) Reach over with your right hand, and grab his right wrist, pinning it to your chest. (3) Pull him off bal-

3

ance and turn his wrist over so his little finger is up. (4) Apply pressure by bowing forward. This will (5) bring the assailant to his knees.

4

5

Against Lapel Grab Two

(1) Your assailant grabs your lapel with his right hand. (2) Grab his thumb with your right hand so you can compress the first knuckle. (3) Peel the hand off your lapel by compressing his first knuckle of his thumb. Continue the pressure until he submits.

Against High Reach One

To apply the small-circle arm bar counter to a high reach, (1&2) keep the assailant's elbow turned upward as you drive your fore-knuckles into the tricep tendon. (3) Step back as you continue to drive the knuckles down and keep his wrist anchored to your shoulder. This will bring him to the ground face down.

Against High Reach Two

(1) If the attacker's arm is bent as he reaches high, (2) plant your right radial bone on the tricep tendon and then turn the elbow upward. (3) Grab your own hand with your lefty hand, and apply slow downward pressure on the tendon. Keep the wrist anchored on your shoulder for control.

Against Front Bear Hug One

(1) You are held in a front bear hug with your arms pinned to your sides. (2) Drive your right knee into his groin. (3) Hook your right leg inside his left knee to ob-

struct his left leg from stepping back, then (4) lunge forward and take the assailant down on his back. (5) Once he is down, drive your knee into his groin.

Against Front Bear Hug Two

(1&2) Your assailant bear hugs you from the front. (3&4) Drive your foreknuckles into his floating ribs to move him away from you. (5&6) Bring your right arm under his left arm trapping his left forearm against your back, and press the edge of your right hand across his sternum so that your forearm applies pressure to the tricep tendon. In practice, be sure to apply the small-circle wrist extension slowly or you will break the joint.

1

4

3

6

Against Rear Bear Hug

(1) You are attacked with a rear bear hug, arms pinned to your sides. (2&3) Step out with your right foot to shift your hips and drive your palm up into his groin. (4&5) Slip your left leg behind his hips. (6) Sweep counterclockwise with your left arm under his armpit to take him down.

3

6

1

2

Against Belt Grab

As your assailant (1) tries to grab you for a hip throw, (2) bring your left arm under his right arm, and grab his lapel as high as possible. (3&4) Apply the small-circle wrist extension with your left hand as you pin his arm to your body with your left biceps. This will drive your forearm into the tricep tendon, and keep him under control.

3

4

Against Neck Grab

(1) The assailant grabs your neck with his left hand, and pulls his right fist back to strike you. (2) As he does this, plant your right radial bone on his left tricep tendon, and roll his elbow over.

(3) Grab on top of your right fist with your left hand. (4) Drive your radial bone into his tricep tendon as you press upward with your shoulder for control.

Against Flying Tackle

(1) Your assailant tries to tackle you. (2) Move to his outside and press down on his head with your left hand. Keep his momentum going by scooping up his left arm with your right arm. (3) Push his head down and pull his arm up to roll him to the ground.

Against Being Straddled With Arms Pinned

(1) In a prone position, you are straddled by your assailant who has pinned your arms by the wrists. (2) Press up hard with your arms. As the assailant responds by leaning his weight forward pressing harder on your wrists, (3) suddenly swing your arms down to your sides and simultaneously buck your hips upward. This will topple him head first over you. Then, (4&5) turn and strike to his groin.

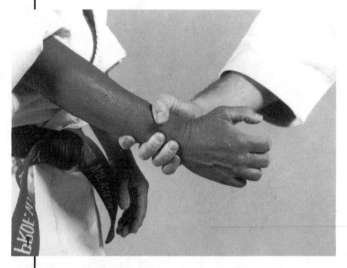

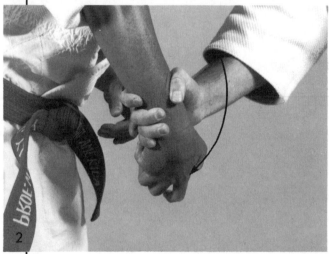

Inside Release Escape

(1) The assailant grabs your right wrist with his right hand. His grip is weak between hiis thumb and index finger. (2) Apply small-circle wrist extension to offset his

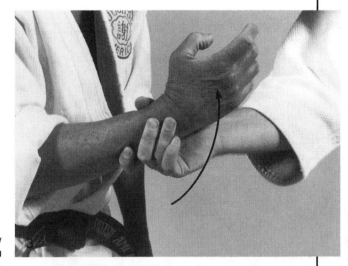

grip. (3&4) Move your elbow toward his centerline as you bring your hand back toward your own head. This will create the leverage to escape his grip.

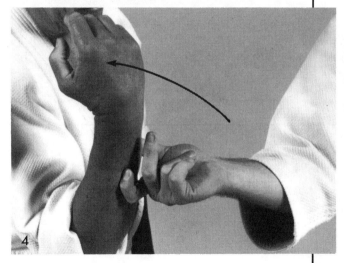

1

2

Outside Release Escape

(1) The assailant grabs your right wrist with his right hand. (2) Rotate your hand clockwise around his wrist. (3) Anchor his right wrist by pinning his right hand with

your left hand. (4&5) Curl the fingers of your right hand around his wrist, and apply pressure downward and in toward his centerline.

Between Thumb and Finger Release

(1) Your assailant grabs your right wrist with his right hand. (2) Catch his wrist between your thumb and index finger. (3) Move to his outside and grab his wrist with your left hand. (4&5) Roll your left elbow over his arm and apply pressure just above his elbow with your armpit in a reverse arm bar.

Wedge Out Release on Opposite Side Hold

(1) Your assailant grabs the outside of your left wrist with his right hand. (2) Step to his outside as you press your left elbow toward his right forearm. This will create leverage between his thumb and index finger and (3) release the hold.

238

2

4

5

2

3

Escape From Two Hands Holding One

(1) The assailant used two hands to grab your right wrist. (2) Grab your own right hand with your left hand, and (3-5) drive your right

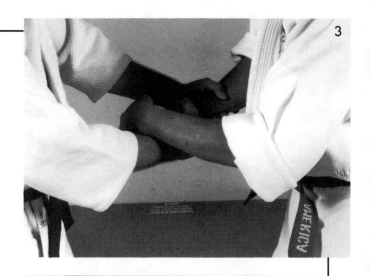

elbow directly toward your assailant's centerline as you pull your right hand with your left back toward you.

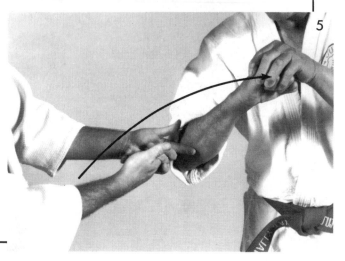

Overhand Wrist Grab Release

(1) The assailant grabs both of your wrists. (2) Raise your knuckles up. (3) Bring your hands together sharply, and drive the back of the assailant's hands into each other. The pain will cause him to release the grip.

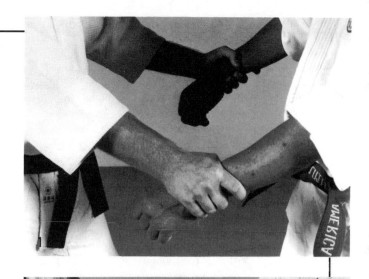

Double Hand Grab Release

(1) The assailant grabs both of your wrists. (2) Rotate your right fist so your palm faces up. (3) Drive your palm down so the back of the assailant's left hand is driven against the knuckle of his thumb. This nerve attack will release the hold.

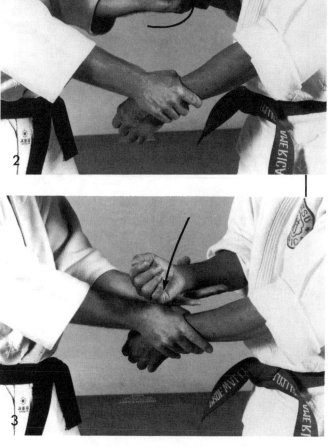

243

1

Overhand Wrist Grab Counter

(1) Face your assailant in a ready position. (2) He grabs both your wrists on the outside. (3) Counter by grabbing his wrists, your palms on top of his radial bones, and pull down to throw him off balance. (4) Drive his left arm under his right elbow. (5&6) Spin counterclockwise. (7) Pull with your left hand and push with your right to throw him on his back. In training, release your partner's right hand so he can fall safely.

3

6

5

Underhand Wrist Lock Against Two Hand Grab

(1) The assailant grabs both your wrists on the outsides. (2) Rotate your palms up and bring your right hand under your left. (3) Reach up with your right hand and grab the thumb pad of the assailant's right hand. Use leverage to break his right hand hold on your left wrist. (4)

4

Apply the small-circle extension with your right hand by pulling with your fingers and pushing with your thumb to drive his right elbow to his centerline. (5&6) Use your left hand to help press down on his right wrist for a takedown.

5

6

Pull Away and Side Kick

(1) The assailant grabs your wrist and attempts to pull you. (2) Resist his pull at first by squatting low. As he pulls harder, suddenly go with his force and (3&4) drive a low side kick into the side of his

knee joint. Step through with your kick, and you will inflict severe mechanical injury to his knee. The pain will force him to release his hold.

3

4

1

2

Countering an Arm Bar With a Shoulder Throw

Your assailant (1) attempts to apply a regular arm bar to your right arm. (2) Use your left hand to push up on your right hand. (3) Lower your hips and shift them to the

right as you pull forward with your arms and straighten your legs. This will (4&5) throw the assailant over your shoulder.

Countering an Arm Bar
With an Arm Lock

The assailant (1) attemps to apply a regular arm bar to your right arm. (2) Use your left hand to push up on your right hand as you move your hips down and to the right. (3&4) Continue turning to the left as you pivot 360 degrees. (5&6) This locks your left forearm under the tricep tendon so your radial bone can drive in.

3

6

Countering a Counter to an Arm Bar

(1) As you move to apply a regular arm bar, the assailant (2) bends his arm to counter you. (3) Blend with his force and roll his elbow over so that it is placed under your armpit. (4&5)

3

Push down with your armpit on the tricep tendon as you pull up on the assailant's wrist. Remember that the push/pull motion is simultaneous.

4

5